I0406835

COPYRIGHT

Foundations
Presents

GEORGE **D. DELVIN**

DEDICATION

This book is for everyone who has ever felt the impacts of overwork, burnout, or doing work that lacks purpose since we live in a culture that values work above everything else. Don't feel bad about deserving better; you're not alone. To everyone who wants to live a life where work is not a chore but a source of meaning and pleasure: this book is for you. You are sane and capable of altering your behavior.

Charles C. Alvadon and **Cornel W. Brown**, two of my coworkers at **DIC Foundations**, have been very helpful and inspirational to me during this work. They have been crucial in raising my frequency and spreading my message. I feel very blessed to be a member of this extraordinary organization that is working to assist humanity in ascending to greater levels of awareness and existence.

In addition, I appreciate the support, understanding, and love of my loved ones and the people who read my work. You have been my inspiration and driving force during this ordeal. I pray that this book will be an invaluable resource in realizing your ambitions.

Ultimately, all we want is more time to devote to the people and things that matter to us. In such a situation, you need to slow down, relax, and enjoy life a little more.

Table of Content

The Workaholic Dilemma:
Exposing the Productivity Illusion

Consider a world in which no one works. Not a single person. Everyone spends the day at home, watching Netflix, playing video games, or sleeping. Doesn't it sound like paradise? Wrong. It'd be a nightmare. A catastrophe of epic proportions. What would happen if we all quit working?

- The economy would implode. Nobody would manufacture, trade, or purchase anything. The money would lose its value. Banks would close. Companies would go bankrupt. The infrastructure would fall apart. Nobody would keep the roads, bridges, railroads, airports, or power plants running. The power, water, gas, and internet would be turned off. It would be difficult to communicate.

- Society would disintegrate. Nobody would offer basic services like health care, education, law enforcement, or firefighting. Without assistance, people would get ill, wounded, or dead. The level of crime and violence would soar.

- The environment would suffer as a result. Nobody cares about animals, plants, or natural resources. Pollution and garbage would accumulate. Climate change would accelerate.

In a nutshell, we'd be doomed. Work is essential to our existence and well-being. Work is the only thing that keeps us alive and civilized.

But wait a second. Does this imply that we must labor constantly? Does this imply that we must forego our pleasure and freedom to work? Is this to imply that we have no option but to accept the status quo?

No way! There is another way to live. A method of balancing work and relaxation. A method to enjoy the results of our labor without exhausting ourselves. A method that allows us to devote more time to ourselves and our loved ones.

That is the matter of this book. It's all about determining the ideal quantity of work for you and your lifestyle. It is about identifying your life passion and purpose. It is about fostering a workplace culture that recognizes your needs and ideals.

How do we go about it? It's not going to be easy. It requires some experimenting and creativity. It takes some bravery and adaptability. It takes foresight and action.

But it's also not impossible. In reality, several governments have already begun to work towards this aim. They have attempted to reduce the work week from five to four days. What's more, guess what? The results are stunning.

Here are some of the advantages of working four days a week:

- Boosted production and efficiency. Workers may concentrate better on their duties and prevent distractions and mistakes by working fewer hours. They may also save money and time on commuting and other costs.

- Better health and well-being. Workers may lower their stress levels and enhance their mental and physical health by working less. They may also help to avoid burnout and tiredness.

- Increased creative and innovative thinking. Workers with greater free time might pursue hobbies and interests, as well as learn new skills and ideas.

- Improved ties and community. Workers may increase their social and emotional support and happiness by spending more time with their family and friends.
- Less of an environmental effect. Workers may help to make the world a more sustainable and eco-friendly place by using fewer resources and creating less trash.

Sounds too good to be true, doesn't it? It's not a fantasy, after all. It is a reality in places such as New Zealand, Spain, and Iceland. They have undertaken experiments in which a four-day work week was adopted in several industries and organizations. And they've discovered that both employees and companies benefit from it.

A four-day work week, of course, is not a one-size-fits-all answer for everyone or every scenario. Making such a drastic adjustment has both advantages and disadvantages. There are also other approaches to designing and implementing a four-day workweek. That is why we must go further into this subject and learn from the experiences of others. That is what this book will assist you with.

1st

Chapter

Rest More, Wrok Less

1st Chapter

Rest as Radical Rebellion: Defying the Establishment

Iceland is one of the nations that has made news for its work experiments. Between 2015 and 2019, the island country conducted a series of experiments in which they reduced the work week from five to four days. The trials included around 2,500 people from different industries and organizations. What's more, guess what? They lost no money or production. They maintained their salary and production constant.

But it isn't all. They also earned something invaluable: pleasure. Employees reported increased levels of happiness, well-being, and health. They reported feeling less anxious, fatigued, and burnt out. They had more time and energy to devote to their interests, families, and communities. They just had a better time in life.

How did they manage it? It wasn't magic, after all. It was the result of careful preparation, adaptable management, and collaborative cooperation. The employees and their managers reached an agreement on how to reorganize their schedules, duties, and objectives. They got rid of all the needless meetings, emails, and paperwork. They prioritized quality over quantity.

The outcomes were so striking that they ignited a countrywide movement. Because of union and public demand, more than 80% of Iceland's workforce now has access to shorter or more flexible work hours. Even the suits in the business sector are pleased since they save money on overhead without losing performance.

That is a remarkable success for a nation that used to have among of Europe's longest working hours. But why should we stop there? Why not take it a step further?

It's about questioning the beliefs and practices that guide our workplace culture. It's about exploring tough questions about work, its purpose, and its influence on our lives. It is about investigating the potential and advantages of working less and living more.

Some of these inquiries include:

- Why do we put forth so much effort? What historical, economic, and societal influences determine our work ethic and expectations?

- What are the costs and effects of working too much? What are the consequences for our physical, mental, emotional, and environmental health?

- What alternatives exist to the existing work model? How can we create and implement a working system that takes into account our needs and values?

- How can we overcome the obstacles and problems that come with working less? What are the political, societal, and psychological barriers to altering our work habits?

- What can we do with our spare time? How can we utilize it to pursue our interests, passions, and goals?

These are difficult questions to address. They need some investigation, analysis, and contemplation. They also need bravery, imagination, and action.

They are not, however, impossible questions. Indeed, several governments have begun to address them in different ways. They have tried lowering or reorganizing their work hours in various settings and scenarios. And they've discovered that both employees and companies benefit from it.

Here are some nations that have attempted or are attempting to implement a shorter or more flexible work week:

New Zealand: Perpetual Guardian conducted an experiment in which they decreased their work week from 40 to 32 hours without reducing salary or output. Employees reported increased levels of engagement, drive, and equilibrium.

- Spain: The government launched a trial initiative in which enterprises would be subsidized if they decrease their work week from 40 to 32 hours without harming income or employment. The goal is to increase employment, productivity, and overall well-being.

- Japan: Several organizations have implemented a "morning person" policy, which allows workers to begin and end their workdays earlier than normal. The objective is to boost productivity, health, and work-life balance.

- Sweden: Several towns and organizations have experimented with a six-hour workday with full compensation for their employees. The outcomes demonstrated better service quality, employee morale, and customer satisfaction.

- Germany: A metalworkers' trade union reached an agreement with employers that allows them to cut their work week from 35 to 28 hours for up to two years for personal reasons such as family care or study.

Since 2000, France has had a legal restriction of 35 hours per week for most jobs. The legislation intends to boost job creation, decrease unemployment, and enhance leisure time.

These are just a few instances of how many nations are experimenting with new methods of doing things. There are many more situations throughout the globe from which we may learn.

OTHER ADVANTAGES OF A SHORTENED WORKWEEK INCLUDE:

Companies may save money on overhead expenditures such as energy, water, heating, and cooling by working fewer hours. They may also help to cut down on absenteeism, turnover, and recruiting expenses.

Employee cost savings: By working fewer hours, workers may save money on commuting, childcare, food, and clothes. They may also avoid paying taxes on additional income or overtime.

Employees may lower their carbon footprint and environmental effect by working less. They may consume less fuel, produce less trash, and release fewer greenhouse emissions.

Improved work-life balance: By working fewer hours, people may strike a better balance between their professional and personal lives. They will have more time to devote to their hobbies, interests, and ambitions. They will also have more time to spend with their family and friends.

Employee pleasure and satisfaction may be increased by working less. Their employers may make them feel more valued, respected, and appreciated. They may also have more independence, flexibility, and control over their job.

Employee well-being improves: By working fewer hours, workers may enhance their physical and emotional health. They can lessen their tension and avoid burnout and tiredness. They may also help to prevent or treat chronic illnesses including obesity, diabetes, heart disease, and depression.

Increased productivity: Employees may boost their productivity and efficiency by working fewer hours. They can concentrate better on their duties and avoid distractions and mistakes. They may also work on their creativity and ingenuity.

Attracting job candidates: Companies may attract more qualified and competent job applicants by providing a shorter work week. They may also keep their current personnel and decrease turnover.

Better time management and job prioritization: Working fewer hours teaches people how to better manage their time and prioritize their work. They may reduce low-value or needless tasks and concentrate on high-value or high-impact activities.

These are some of the advantages of a shorter work week as documented by many research and trials conducted throughout the globe. Of course, various perks and downsides may exist depending on the setting and condition of each organization or individual. That is why, before introducing a shortened work week, it is critical to thoroughly weigh the benefits and drawbacks.

If you wish to persuade your coworkers to embrace a four-day workweek, try the following steps:

- Do your study: Before approaching your coworkers, make sure you've done some research on the pros and drawbacks of a four-day workweek. You may utilize the sources I mentioned in my earlier response or hunt for further information from credible sites. You should also be prepared to answer any possible issues or objections raised by your colleagues, such as how it would impact your workload, deadlines, clients, or money.

- Perform a personal experiment: One method to illustrate the feasibility and usefulness of a four-day workweek is to try it for some time yourself. You may request permission from your manager to work four days a week for a month or two and measure your productivity, well-being, and satisfaction levels. You may also keep track of any problems or issues you face and how you overcome them. You may use these statistics to back up your argument and demonstrate to your colleagues the benefits of a four-day workweek on your performance and satisfaction.

- Determine their interest: You may be wondering if your colleagues would be interested in a four-day workweek. Begin by pitching your concept to a small group of trusted peers to measure their interest. Share your findings and see how others respond. If their reaction is positive, you may want to urge them to attempt the experiment themselves. You may also solicit opinions and recommendations from them on how to enhance or modify your plan.

- Create a coalition: Once you have some supporters for your proposal, you may attempt to broaden your network and reach out to other colleagues who may be interested or open-minded. To spread the word and ask people to join your cause, you may utilize word-of-mouth, e-mails, newsletters, or social media. You may also hold seminars, workshops, or webinars to educate and enlighten your coworkers on the advantages and disadvantages of a four-day workweek. You may also include examples, testimonies, or anecdotes from other firms or nations that have successfully adopted a four-day workweek.

- Present a formal proposal: Once you've gathered a large number of supporters, you may make a formal presentation to your supervisor or senior management. Make certain that your proposal is precise, simple, and appealing. You should emphasize the advantages of a four-day workweek for both individuals and the organization, such as greater productivity, cost savings, better health, more creativity, and higher retention. You should also explain any possible dangers or disadvantages, as well as how you intend to minimize them. You should also provide a timetable and budget for adopting and assessing the four-day workweek.

These are some actions you may take to persuade your coworkers to embrace a four-day week off Of course, there's no assurance that you'll persuade everyone or get permission from your supervisor or management. However, by following these steps, you may improve your chances of bringing about a good change in your workplace culture and environment.

2nd Chapter

The Burnout Epidemic: Unravelling Overwork's Consequences

We often hear, "We need to get back to work." Our employees are eager to return to their offices, factories, and stores. They miss their jobs and coworkers. They want to make a livelihood and give back to society. Work is more than simply a means of earning money. It gives you a sense of pride, identity, and belonging. That is why none of the main political parties in the United States is advocating for a drastic decrease in work hours. They understand the significance of work in our well-being and happiness.

Is this, however, true? Do we all like our work so much that we want more time doing them? Is our job meaningful, satisfying, and enjoyable for all of us? Do we all appreciate the working circumstances, expectations, and demands?

No, it does not. It's not even close. According to a Gallup study conducted in 2019, just 34% of U.S. employees are engaged at work, which means they are passionate, devoted, and interested in their jobs. The remaining 52% are either not involved (52% are indifferent, distant, or bored) or actively disengaged (13% are dissatisfied, resentful, or angry). That's a lot of folks that are dissatisfied with their work or their employers.

It's not merely an issue of personal taste or attitude. Working too much or too little has actual costs and consequences. Overwork may cause stress, burnout, depression, anxiety, sleeplessness, obesity, diabetes, heart disease, and stroke, among other things. It may also harm our relationships, the environment, and society.

So why are we putting up with it? Why do we continue to work long hours for poor compensation and little satisfaction? Why don't we expect more from our jobs and employers? Why not question the rules and assumptions that control our workplace culture?

It's a choice between being against or for work. But what exactly does it mean?

It does not imply laziness or selfishness. It does not imply dismissing the importance or need of employment. It does not imply a desire to live off the government or the labor of others.

IT HAS A DIFFERENT MEANING. THIS MEANS:

- Recognizing that labor is a means to an aim rather than an end in itself.
- Recognizing that work is not the only or best means to attain our dreams and ambitions.
- Inquiring about the amount and quality of work that we perform and are expected to accomplish.
- Investigating alternatives and ideas for working less and better.
- Seeking a balance between our commitments and our hobbies, between our job and our leisure.
- Demanding more from our jobs and employers, such as fair compensation, acceptable working conditions, flexible hours, and meaningful employment.
- Developing a work environment that honors our needs and ideals, such as individuality, creativity, variety, and unity.

These are some of the implications of being against or anti-work. There is, of course, more to it than that. There are several points of view and approaches to this subject. There are also several difficulties and barriers to overcome.

There is, however, hope and opportunity. Other nations and businesses who have tried or are attempting innovative methods of working have provided proof and experience. There is room for improvement and development.

Burnout is setting in.

You are not alone if you are fatigued, pessimistic, and useless at work. Burnout is a prolonged condition of stress that may have major effects on your health, happiness, and performance.

Burnout is not a new issue. It was initially defined in the 1970s by psychologist Herbert Freudenberger as a disorder affecting individuals who are committed to their profession but feel disillusioned and overwhelmed by it. Since then, the World Health Organization has recognized burnout as an occupational phenomenon that may lead to physical and mental illnesses such as depression, anxiety, sleeplessness, heart disease, and stroke.

However, burnout is not only a personal issue. It is also an organizational issue. According to a 2021 research conducted by Harvard Business Review, more than 80% of employees polled reported feeling burnt out at work, with more than half reporting feeling burned out all or most of the time. Millions of employees have experienced greater workloads, longer hours, blurred boundaries, isolation, and uncertainty as a result of the epidemic.

The expenses of burnout are enormous. Burnout may lower productivity, creativity, and job quality. It has the potential to increase absenteeism, turnover, and mistakes. It has the potential to harm relationships, morale, and culture. It may also be harmful to the environment since overworked individuals use more resources and generate more garbage.

So, how can we avoid or overcome burnout? How can we strike a compromise between work closure and the burnout epidemic? How can we work less while living more?

It's all about determining the ideal quantity of work for you and your lifestyle. It is about identifying your life passion and purpose. It is about fostering a workplace culture that recognizes your needs and ideals.

But, before we get to the remedies, let's examine the causes and symptoms of burnout. Let's look at the repercussions of overwork and why it's so difficult to get away.

> Burnout has three dimensions: Burnout is more than just being weary or bored at work. It's a multifaceted condition with three components: emotional weariness (feeling tired and depleted), depersonalization (feeling

distant and cynical), and decreased personal achievement (feeling useless and inadequate).

The following are the six causes of burnout: Workload (having too much or too little to do), control (having too little or too much autonomy), reward (having insufficient or inappropriate recognition), community (having poor or conflicting relationships), fairness (having unfair or unclear policies), and values (having mismatched or unclear goals) are all factors that contribute to burnout.

Burnout symptoms and stages: Burnout does not occur suddenly, but rather progressively over time. It may show in a variety of ways depending on the individual and the environment.

Physical symptoms (such as headaches, fatigue, insomnia, or illness), emotional symptoms (such as irritability, apathy, anger, or sadness), behavioral symptoms (such as procrastination, withdrawal, cynicism, or substance abuse), cognitive symptoms (such as memory loss, concentration problems, or poor judgment), and motivational symptoms (such as lack of interest, enthusiasm, or satisfaction) are some common signs of burnout. Burnout may also go through many phases, such as excitement, stagnation, frustration, and indifference.

Burnout's implications: Burnout may have major repercussions for our health, happiness, performance, relationships, society, and the environment. Burnout increases our chances of getting physical and mental disorders including cardiovascular disease, diabetes, depression, anxiety, or post-traumatic stress disorder.

Burnout may reduce our life satisfaction, happiness, well-being, and sense of purpose. Burnout may hurt our productivity, creativity, quality, and efficiency. Burnout may harm our communication, cooperation, trust, and loyalty. Burnout may exacerbate societal issues such as inequality, violence, crime, or corruption. Burnout may also be harmful to the environment because overworked individuals use more resources and generate more garbage.

Solutions

- Assess your burnout level and risk factors: You may assess your burnout level and uncover the elements that contribute to it using numerous tools and tests. You may also utilize self-reflection and feedback to obtain a better understanding of your condition and requirements.

- Change your perspective and habits: You may take a more optimistic and proactive approach to your job and life. You may also cultivate healthier and more productive habits such as establishing boundaries, managing your time, prioritizing your duties, delegating your job, asking for assistance, saying no, taking breaks, practicing gratitude, celebrating your successes, and learning from your disappointments.

- Seek assistance and resources: You may get aid from a variety of people, including family, friends, coworkers, mentors, coaches, counselors, or therapists. You may also get access to books, podcasts, blogs, courses, seminars, and webinars.

You may advocate for change and action on behalf of yourself and others who are suffering from burnout. You may also take steps to enhance your workplace's culture and atmosphere. You may bargain for better terms, such as fair compensation, flexible working hours, meaningful responsibilities, or recognition. You may also join or start movements that promote workplace well-being and happiness.

You may balance your job closing with the burnout pandemic by following these procedures. It is possible to work less and live more. You may find fulfillment and meaning in your profession and your life.

3rd
Chapter

Rest More, Wrok Less

3rd Chapter

The Work Paradox: Why We Love and Hate It in Capitalism

Work is something that we must all do, whether we like it or not. It's how we make a livelihood, pay our bills, and purchase things. It is also how we contribute to society, express ourselves, and reach our full potential. Work may provide us pleasure, pride, and fulfillment. It may, however, be a cause of sadness, worry, and frustration.

Why is work such a jumbled mess? Why do we have such conflicting emotions about it? The explanation lies in labor under capitalism, the economic system that now governs the majority of the globe.

Capitalism is founded on the private ownership of productive assets such as land, factories, machinery, and tools. These are held by a small group of individuals known as capitalists or company owners, who utilize them to profitably manufacture products and services. The bulk of individuals, referred to as employees or workers, do not own the means of production. In return for salaries, they must sell their labor capacity to capitalists.

As a result, the two classes have a basic conflict of interest. Capitalists want to maximize profits by paying employees as little as possible while forcing them to work as much as possible. Workers strive to maximize their earnings by earning as much as possible while working as little as feasible.

In the workplace, this conflict manifests itself in a variety of ways. As an example:

Capitalists attempt to exert control over employees' time, duties, and production. They determine the working hours, deadlines, and quotas. They supervise, appraise, and reprimand the employees. They establish policies, rules, and regulations.

Workers attempt to oppose the capitalist rule. They want pay increases, perks, and bonuses. They organize unions, strike, or sabotage production. They violate the rules, take their time, or quit.

As a consequence, there is a perpetual conflict between exploitation and resistance, dominance and revolt.

However, there is more to the job than this tangible component. Work includes a psychological and social component. Work has an impact on how we think, feel, and interact with ourselves and others.

Work has a detrimental influence on our psychological and social well-being under capitalism. This is because capitalism separates us from our job, ourselves, our coworkers, and our society.

Alienation is the separation from anything that belongs to us or to which we belong. It entails losing control over something that is a part of us or of which we are a part. It is feeling disconnected from something important to us or to which we are important.

Under capitalism, we are cut off from:

Our work: We have no control over what we do or how we do it. We don't like or recognize the value in what we do. We do not own what we make, nor do we profit from it. We are simply concerned about being compensated for our efforts.

We do not cultivate our abilities or hobbies. We don't show our personalities or originality. We do not realize our full potential or attain our objectives. We simply care about survival and eating.

We do not cooperate or collaborate with our coworkers. We do not believe or support them. We don't care about them or sympathize with them. We merely compete or disagree with them.

We do not engage in or contribute to our society. We don't comprehend it or have any control over it. We don't fit in or identify with it. We simply have two options: comply or resist it.

We feel sad, unsatisfied, disappointed, furious, depressed, nervous, lonely, alienated, hopeless, and meaningless as a result of these types of estrangement.

So, why are we putting up with this? Why don't we do anything about it? Why don't we invent a new sort of employment and a new kind of society?

Why do we put forth so much effort? What historical, economic, and societal influences determine our work ethic and expectations?

What are the costs and effects of working too much? How does it affect our physical, mental, emotional, and environmental health, as well as our relationships, happiness, and meaning?

What alternatives exist to the existing work model? How can we create and implement a working system that takes into account our needs and values?

How can we overcome the obstacles and problems that come with working less? What are the political, cultural, and psychological barriers to altering our working habits?

What can we do with our spare time? How can we utilize it to pursue our interests, passions, and goals?

These are difficult questions to address. They need some investigation, analysis, and contemplation. They also need bravery, imagination, and action.

They are not, however, impossible questions. Indeed, some individuals have begun to confront them in different ways. They have tried lowering or reorganizing their work hours in various settings and scenarios. And they have discovered favorable benefits for themselves as well as their organizations.

Here are some instances of persons who have attempted or are now attempting a new method of working:

Tim Ferriss, the best-selling author of The 4-Hour Workweek, explains how to escape the 9-to-5 rat race and live anywhere while working remotely and outsourcing duties.

Jennifer Moss, the author of The Burnout Epidemic, a book that explains the true causes of burnout and how organizations may break the chronic stress cycle that afflicts an increasing number of employees.

Andrew Barnes, the founder of Perpetual Guardian, a New Zealand financial services firm that transitioned its 240 employees from a five-day to a four-day work week in 2018 while retaining their salary.

Ricardo Semler, the CEO of Semco, a Brazilian corporation that practices radical democracy and self-management by enabling employees to pick their own working hours, salary, and supervisors.

Cal Newport, the author of Deep Labour, a book that argues for the value of continuous, concentrated labor in a world of frequent distractions and superficial activities.

These are just a few instances of how individuals are experimenting with new methods of working.

THE EVOLUTION OF WORK IN AMERICA

Work in America has a history of change, struggle, and variety. It represents the nation's and its people's economic, social, and political transitions. It also highlights the hardships and accomplishments of people who have worked to better their lives and working circumstances.

Work in America has been classified into four major periods:

- The colonial era (1607-1776) saw European immigrants create colonies in North America, mostly along the Atlantic coast. Agriculture, commerce, and crafts were the foundations of the economy. The majority of the laborers were farmers, craftsmen, or indentured slaves who labored for a certain period in return for passage to America. Some laborers were enslaved Africans who were compelled to work on plantations or in houses after being transported to America against their choice. Work was governed by tradition, religion, and the law. Workers had few rights or safeguards, although some established groups or unions to advocate for their rights.

- The early national era (1776-1849) saw the United States acquire independence from Britain and extend its territory westward. Agriculture continued to dominate the economy, but trade, industry, and transportation also grew in importance. New technologies, such as the steam engine, cotton gin, and railroad, improved output and linked disparate places. Many employees moved from rural to urban or frontier regions in quest of better possibilities. Some employees were wage earners who offered their labor to employers for a fee. Others were Africans who were slaves and denied their freedom and human rights. Market dynamics, political movements, and social changes all had an impact on the work. Workers faced difficulties such as poor earnings, long hours, hazardous working conditions, and discrimination. Some employees organized strikes, rallies, or political parties to seek better working conditions or reforms.

- The industrial era (1849-1945) saw the United States emerge as a global power and industrialization leader. Large-scale manufacturing, mass consumption, and global commerce drove the economy. Steel, oil, electricity, and vehicles were among the new industries that arose and altered society. People worked in factories, mines, mills, and offices. Many laborers were immigrants from Europe or Asia seeking a better life in America. Some of the employees were women or children who were making their first forays into the labor field. Innovation, competition, and regulation all had an impact on the workplace. Workers faced difficulties such as exploitation, insecurity, and war. To negotiate collectively or act politically, some employees created unions, federations, or coalitions.

- The postwar era (1945-present): This was the period in which the United States established itself as a powerhouse and a leader in information technology. Services, knowledge, and innovation were the foundations of the economy. New sectors expanded and diversified society, such as health care, education, entertainment, and finance. Millions of people worked in professional, technical, or creative jobs. Many employees were minorities, women, or immigrants who expanded their labor-force participation and representation. Globalization, digitalization, and diversification have had an impact on the workplace. Workers were confronted with issues such as automation, outsourcing, and inequality. Some workers established networks, movements, or platforms to cooperate, communicate, or advocate.

These are some of the most important aspects of American labor history. There is, of course, more to it than that. Several viewpoints and experiences might help us better comprehend labor and its significance in American society.

This investigates the contradiction of labor under capitalism, in which employment is both essential and alienating, meaningful and unhappy. It investigates the historical, economic, and social elements that influence our work ethic and expectations, as well as the costs and repercussions of overworking for our health, happiness, performance, relationships, society, and planet. It also poses some concerns and provides examples of how to challenge the present work paradigm and develop alternatives that are respectful of our needs and beliefs.

4th

Chapter

Rest More, Wrok Less

4th Chapter

How to Break Free from the Boring Work You Hate and Find Work You Love

Do you ever find yourself questioning your career path? Have you ever felt that your life lacked purpose and you wished you could change that?

If you identified with any of the above, know that you are not alone. Gallup found that just 15% of the world's workforce is "engaged," or fully passionate, devoted, and active in their jobs. The other 18% are either actively disengaged because they are angry, resentful, or hostile, or passively disengaged because they are apathetic, disconnected, or bored (67%).

That translates to 8 out of 10 people not enjoying their professions. That's a lot of folks that hate what they do for a living and feel hopeless about their situation.

To what end, though? For what reason do so many believe their workdays are pointless? And what recourse do they have?

The disconnect between our actions and our beliefs lies at the heart of pointless labor. The capitalist system in which we operate places a premium on quantity over quality, efficiency over originality, and money above everything else. Many of us have jobs at companies that don't value us as individuals or our unique set of skills and interests. We adhere to regulations, norms, and policies that seldom make any sense or advance the greater good. We create things that don't always help anybody or address any pressing issue.

In a nutshell, we engage in activities that aren't in line with who we are or what we want to achieve. We're stuck in jobs that don't inspire us or help us grow. Our jobs don't provide us with any sense of satisfaction or enjoyment.

And to make things worse, we are often required to act as if we are enthusiastic about our job when, in reality, we are not. Even if we aren't, we need to give the impression that we are busy, productive, and driven. We have to act as though we're successful even when we know deep down that we aren't.

This leads to an endless loop of boredom and anger. Our jobs are boring since they don't provide enough stimulation or challenge for us. We're dissatisfied with the lack of appreciation and appreciation for our efforts. Because of the limitations imposed by our jobs, we often feel stuck in a rut.

And this loop has devastating effects on our health. Anxiety, despair, sleeplessness, disease, and even suicide have all been linked to meaningless labor. Work that lacks purpose may also damage personal connections, communities, and the environment.

What can we do to end this vicious cycle? How can we get out of this rat hole of pointless labor? How can we infuse our work with greater purpose and meaning?

That's the book's main topic. It's all about figuring out how to give our job greater personal significance. Finding methods to incorporate personal interests and ideals into one's professional life is crucial. The goal is to find methods to make the job we do more satisfying and pleasant.

But before we get to the answers, let's examine the issue at hand. Let's break down the effects of pointless labor and figure out why we can't seem to escape it.

- Meaninglessness at work in all its forms: It's not only being weary or bored at work that constitutes meaningless labor. It's a multifaceted problem with four main causes: dissatisfaction with one's work's significance, competence, autonomy, and relatedness.

- The root reasons for pointless labor: Organizational (including culture, structure, leadership, strategy, goals, policies, processes, rewards, feedback, etc.), personal (including values, interests, strengths, weaknesses, expectations, motivations, etc.), and environmental (including market, industry, economy, society) factors all contribute to our perception of whether or not our work is meaningful.

- Here are some telltale indications of pointless labor: Work that lacks meaning develops slowly but steadily over time. Depending on the individual and the circumstances, it may present itself in a variety of ways. Physical symptoms (like headaches, fatigue, insomnia, or illness), emotional symptoms (like irritability, apathy, anger, or sadness), behavioral symptoms (like procrastination, withdrawal, cynicism, or substance abuse), cognitive symptoms (like memory loss, concentration problems, or poor judgment), and motivational symptoms (like lack of interest, enthusiasm, or satisfaction) are all common indicators of meaningless work.

- Work that lacks purpose may have negative effects on health, productivity, relationships, the community, and the environment. Physical and mental health problems including heart disease, diabetes, melancholy, anxiety, and PTSD may all be exacerbated by jobs that don't matter. Work that lacks purpose may harm our efficiency, quality, and output. Our ability to communicate, work together, trust each other, and remain loyal may all be harmed by meaningless tasks. Inequality, violence, crime, and corruption are only some of the societal issues that may be exacerbated by meaningless labor. Those who aren't motivated by their employees are more likely to squander resources and create more trash than those who are.

As you can see, pointless labor is a major issue that has far-reaching consequences. There is, nevertheless, reason for optimism. Avoiding or escaping pointless labor is possible. There are methods to infuse greater purpose and fulfillment into what we do each day.

You may avoid being trapped in useless labor by following these guidelines. You have the power to infuse your job with deeper purpose and enjoyment. Work and life may provide you satisfaction and meaning.

An In-Depth Guide to Finding Fulfillment in Your Career

So, you've come to terms with the fact that your job is pointless and are determined to change that. That's fantastic! You've already accomplished the first step toward a more positive and rewarding working experience. And now what? How can you shift your mood from one of boredom and frustration to one of engagement and contentment?

The goal is to provide you with actionable advice and resources that will make your job more fulfilling. The goal is to assist you in pinpointing your "sweet spot," the point at which your professional activities most satisfy you.

But before we get into it, I'll share a little bit about my personal experience. Previously, I practiced corporate law at a major company. When I first started working at my current company, I was under the impression that I had made it. But I felt like crap. I hated my job. I was concerned that I was squandering my abilities on something pointless. I didn't feel like I could make decisions or influence my job. I felt completely disconnected from the world and useless.

I couldn't break free from the pattern of useless employment. And I had no idea how to free myself!

And then one day I just stopped doing it. After much thought, I chose to pursue a career in writing. For this reason, I've made it my life's mission to advise others on how to get satisfaction from their careers.

It was a challenge. It put me on edge. The move was perilous. It was arduous. However, the price was justified by the outcome.

Now that I've settled in, I like my job. It now seems like I'm making a difference in the world. I feel like I'm making the most of my abilities. For the most part, I get to decide what I do and how I do it. I'm involved and feel like my efforts are making a difference.

I've finally discovered my niche. So can you. Here are some things you may do to bring greater purpose and fulfillment to your work:

- Evaluate the significance and potential dangers: The first thing to do is take stock of your current situation and set some goals for the future. You may assess your degree of meaning and the elements that contribute to it with the use of a variety of instruments and examinations. Take the Meaningful Work Questionnaire to find out how much meaning, mastery, independence, and connection you have at work. Self-reflection and criticism may also help you better understand your circumstances and requirements.

Some thoughts to ponder include: "What do I value most in life?" Where do my interests and passions lie? Who am I, and what do I need to work on? What do I want to accomplish with my life? Where can I get the inspiration for my artwork? Where does the lack of significance in my efforts come from? When I look at my work, how do I feel? What do others think of what I've done thus far?

- The second stage is to adjust your outlook and routines with your job. A more optimistic and assertive outlook on work and life is within your reach. You may raise your degree of meaning by adopting practices that are both physically and mentally beneficial. As an illustration: Limit yourself: Master the art of saying "no" to distractions and unnecessary obligations. Keep your focus and energy on the things that are important to you. Time management Organize your time such that each day, week, month, and year contributes to your long-term objectives. Stay focused and don't get sidetracked by anything that might be avoided.

- Set your priorities: Instead of focusing on what's most urgent or simplest, prioritize what's most critical. Don't waste your time on tasks that don't matter or that you're not good at. Don't be too proud to ask for assistance when you need it. If you need assistance with your work or your interpretation of it, talk to someone who can aid you. Don't overdo it, and give yourself time off to recharge. Relax, refuel, and have some fun at regular intervals throughout the day, week, month, and year.

Appreciate what you do have rather than dwelling on what you don't. Communicate your appreciation to those who have contributed to the success and satisfaction of your endeavors. Rejoice at your success: Give yourself credit for the good job you've done or the successes you've achieved. Tell those who care about you or assist you along the road about your accomplishments.

- The third stage is to look for assistance and tools that may help you discover meaning in your job or increase the degree of meaning you're already experiencing. You may get assistance from: Members of your family who are perhaps the most familiar and caring people in your life. They may provide encouragement, guidance, or constructive criticism. They may also serve to remind you of your principles and interests or to strike a better work-life balance.

All of your pals: Friends are people who understand and appreciate you for who you are and what you stand for in life. They may provide companionship, entertainment, and education. They may also put you in touch with like-minded people who can enrich your job and life. Your coworkers: People you work with have a better chance of understanding your job and its obstacles, or sharing your skills and abilities, than anybody else. In the workplace, they might provide encouragement, guidance, and even criticism. They may also foster an environment of learning and success in the workplace. Mentors are those who have more knowledge or experience than you have, or who have already attained the goals you have set for yourself. They may serve as examples, sources of motivation, or doors to new possibilities. They may also aid in the expansion of one's capabilities and the attainment of one's objectives.

- Your coaches: Your coaches are the individuals in your life who have specific knowledge or experience in guiding others to greater fulfillment in their professional and personal endeavors. They may serve in a therapeutic, counseling, or coaching capacity. They may also aid in making clearer goals and removing obstacles. The tools at your disposal. There are several tools available to you that may assist you in discovering the value and enjoyment of your profession. Books, podcasts, blogs, seminars, workshops, webinars, etc., that guide how to provide greater purpose and satisfaction to your job. These are some examples of places you might look for information: Emily Esfahani Smith's

The Power of Meaning: How to Find Happiness and Fulfillment in an Insatiable Culture Shawn Achor's The Happiness Advantage: How a Positive Mind Powers Your Professional and Personal Success - Daniel H. Pink's Drive: The Unexpected Truth About What Motivates Us Ken Robinson's Finding Your Element: The Proven Path to Fulfillment in Work, Love, and Play - Jeff Goins's The Art of Work is a guide to finding your life's work.

- The fourth phase is to advocate for change and take action to enhance your workplace environment and culture. You can advocate for yourself and others who are trapped in pointless jobs. You have the power to increase your sense of purpose and satisfaction in your job.

If you want to: If you believe that your job lacks significance due to circumstances outside of your control, such as those inside your company or the surrounding environment, you might attempt to bargain for improved working conditions to give your work more significance. You may inquire about increasing your work's relevance, competence, independence, or connectedness, for instance. The workplace may be a place where you can exercise your right to request greater autonomy, freedom, variety, challenge, input, appreciation, reward, etc. If you believe your work is meaningless due to market or industry-specific variables, for example, you might attempt to alter the system or structure that produces meaningless work by either joining an existing movement or starting your own.

You may, for instance, become a part of a group that campaigns for human rights, environmental protection, social equality, etc. The 4-day workweek movement, the meaningful work movement, the positive psychology movement, etc. are all examples of such initiatives aimed at increasing individuals' sense of purpose and satisfaction in their professional lives.

You may increase the value and satisfaction you get from your employment by taking these measures. There isn't a magic bullet that will work for everyone. You need to determine what options are optimal for you and your circumstances. But keep in mind that you are not obligated to accept drudgery. Don't put your skills to use on something that has no chance of succeeding. You don't have to act as if you're interested in your job if you aren't.

You should have much more. You should be compensated fairly for your efforts. You should give your abilities a complete workout. You should be allowed some degree of autonomy and discretion in your job. You have a right to make friends and make a difference in the world.

Your job should provide you with satisfaction and significance. You can.

5th

Chapter

Rest More, Wrok Less

5th Chapter

How to Avoid the "Busy Work Syndrome" and Reclaim Your Life from Pointless Activities

Feeling like life is passing you by and you're simply existing? Do you sometimes wish you could use your skills and abilities in a more fulfilling way?

You have a serious case of being too busy to do anything else. It's the feeling that nothing you do matters and that your life is pointless.

And then, what exactly constitutes busywork? The question is, "Why?"

Any activity that serves no useful purpose is considered busy work. This is meaningless labor that contributes nothing and changes nothing. It's the kind of job that doesn't use your strengths or satisfy your passions. Work like this doesn't provide any sense of satisfaction or enjoyment.

When will we ever learn? Some of the most frequent explanations are as follows:

To get by, we engage in meaningless activities. There are instances when employers, customers, or organizations force us to engage in busy work. They may require us to act in ways that are counterproductive or illogical because of their unreasonable standards, outmoded regulations, or ineffective procedures. They can be doing so to bolster their ego, demonstrate their dominance, or hide their ineptitude.

We engage in meaningless activities on purpose. We may choose to engage in busy work at times.

We might be pushed in the wrong direction by both internal and external factors including the fear of failure, rejection, change, or missing out. It's also possible that we're driven to engage in behavior that ultimately leaves us feeling empty, such as the pursuit of affirmation, recognition, security, or comfort.

In our ignorance, we fill our time with meaningless tasks. Busy work may indeed become second nature. Sometimes we do things without thinking about why or how we learned to do them. We could have stopped short of criticizing the current quo or looking into potential improvements. Without regularly checking in on and updating our vision, we risk drifting off course.

In any case, being too busy is detrimental to our health. It's harmful to our health, productivity, connections, community, and planet. Stress, boredom, frustration, contempt, and indifference are all possible outcomes of an overly demanding workload. Working too much may reduce our efficiency, effectiveness, and even our ability to think creatively. Working too much may harm our relationships with others and reduce our ability to work together effectively.

Societal issues like inequality, violence, crime, and corruption may all be exacerbated by overwork. Workers who are always on the go use more resources and generate more garbage, another way in which hectic work may be detrimental to the environment.

How therefore can we avoid futile activity? Where can we even begin to find employment that matters? How can we make the most of our resources?

THE PRACTICAL GUIDE TO MOVING BEYOND BUSYWORK AND INTO MEANINGFUL WORK

Here are some things you can do instead of filling your time with meaningless activities:

- First, you need to be able to define "busy work" and understand how it is influencing your life. There are several assessments and instruments available to help you determine the extent to which your busy job is affecting your health, productivity, relationships, community, and the planet. To get an idea of how much time you spend on busywork on a daily, weekly, monthly, and yearly basis, you may take a test like the Busy Work Questionnaire.

- Self-reflection and criticism may also help you better understand your circumstances and requirements. Questions such as, "What are the tasks that I do that don't add any value or make any difference?" will help you identify such activities. What activities do I engage in that do not make use of my talents and interests? Which of the things I do each day do not bring me joy or satisfaction? What effects will these activities have on my health, productivity, relationships, community, and the environment?

- The second stage is to minimize or do away with any busy work that may be getting in the way. It is possible to eliminate or reduce the workload by using a variety of methods and procedures. For instance, you may Repetitive, mundane, or low-skill work may be automated with the use of technology or software. Sending emails, updating spreadsheets, and making social media posts are just a few examples of the kinds of chores that may be automated with the help of services like Zapier, IFTTT, and Automate.io.

- The time-consuming, boring, or low-value work might be outsourced to a third party. Tasks like data entry, research, and errand running may all be outsourced using sites like Fiverr, Upwork, and TaskRabbit. Instead of doing something yourself, assign it to someone else whose strengths lie in that area. Tasks like graphic design, report writing, and event planning may all be delegated to colleagues, subordinates, and partners.

- The next stage is to put as much emphasis as possible on prioritizing and optimizing your relevant job. If you want to get more done on the things that are important to you or give you the most satisfaction, you may utilize a variety of strategies and applications to help you do just that. For instance, you may Get your job in line with your values, expertise, and passions. Aligning your job with your mission statement, fundamental beliefs, strengths, interests, and/or purpose are all examples. Take an active interest in what you're doing and give it your all. Incorporate criticism, new information, and creative thinking into your work to make it better. You can become better at what you do by, among other things, reading, learning from others, and experimenting.

Some of the things you can do instead of mindless busywork are listed below. Naturally, no one approach will work for everyone. You need to determine what options are optimal for you and your circumstances.

But keep in mind that you are not obligated to accept busy work. Your efforts need not be wasted on trivial matters. You shouldn't act as if you're too busy to talk.

You should have much more. You should be compensated fairly for your efforts. You should give your abilities a complete workout. You should be allowed some degree of autonomy and discretion in your job. You should reach out to others and give back to the world.

6th
Chapter

Rest More, Wrok Less

6th Chapter

How to Escape the "Hustle Culture" and Reclaim Your Time to Focus on What Really Matters

Do you ever feel like you're putting in too much effort for too little reward? Do you ever feel like you're not living to the fullest because you're so focused on your career? Have you ever believed your efforts were futile or that they weren't making a difference?

You're not alone if you identified with any of these questions. It's a fallacy that you may find more significance in your labors. It's the conviction that your sense of self and your sense of purpose in life are intrinsically linked to your job performance.

Yet, please explain this urban legend. And why do we put our faith in it?

It is a result of our economic system and society that we believe the fiction that more labor equals greater significance. It's a way of life in which money is valued more than people, output is valued over input, and routine is valued above innovation. It's a culture and a system that takes advantage of people by putting them in a constant condition of shortage and uncertainty, requiring them to work excessive hours for inadequate pay. It's a system and culture that keeps employees worried and dissatisfied by making them feel guilty or lazy if they don't work hard enough.

But why do we accept this fiction as truth? Some of the most frequent explanations are as follows:

- We've been conditioned to accept this falsehood as truth. We are conditioned from a young age to believe that our success is determined by our monetary and/or professional achievements. From an early age, we have been inundated with messages encouraging us to put in long hours, keep ourselves occupied, and never give up.

- Our internalization of this myth has led us to believe it. As a society, we have gradually grown to see our sense of worth and fulfillment as directly proportional to our level of success in the workplace. What we do, rather than who we are, has come to define us. Our jobs have become our identities rather than a means to an end.

- Our rationalizations have led us to trust this fallacy. As a defense mechanism against the monotony and stress of our jobs, many of us have started to persuade ourselves that what we do matters. We have convinced ourselves that our efforts are worthwhile and important even when they are not. We have convinced ourselves that our job is worthwhile and gratifying even if we know otherwise.

- For whatever reason, it's not good for us to buy into this notion. It's harmful to our health, productivity, connections, community, and planet. Insomnia, despair, anxiety, sickness, and even suicide are all possible outcomes of buying into this misconception. This fallacy has the potential to reduce our effectiveness, efficiency, and output. Believing this misconception is harmful to our relationships of trust, cooperation, and commitment. Inequality, violence, crime, and corruption are just some of the societal issues that may be exacerbated by a widespread belief in this myth. The ecology suffers when people accept this misconception because they use more resources and create more garbage.

How therefore do we dispel this falsehood? How can we get started making our lives count in ways that matter? How can we make the most of our resources?

A few of you may be confused by my reference to "hustle culture." You may dismiss it as nothing more than a clever use of phrases concocted to increase book sales. Okay, you have a point. It's an attention-grabbing phrase, and I'm banking on it to boost book sales.

The ethos of the hustle is that you must outwork everyone else by working more efficiently and for longer periods. It's the belief that success can be gauged by how hard you work and how much money you make. It's the belief that success in your career requires you to put your health, relationships, interests, and happiness on the back burner.

Although "hustle culture" has been around for a while, it has recently exploded in popularity and intensity as a result of factors such as social media, technological advancements, and globalization. You see it on Instagram with hashtags like #hustleharder and #riseandgrind or #nodaysoff; on YouTube with titles like "How I Made $1 Million in 30 Days" and "How to Work 100 Hours a Week and Still Have Time for Fun"; on podcasts with guests like Gary Vaynerchuk, Tim Ferriss, or Elon Musk, who preach the gospel of hustle and productivity;

on books like The 4-Hour Workweek, The 10X Rule, or Atomic

At first glance, the "hustle culture" may seem to be exciting and motivating. Who wouldn't desire fame, fortune, and respect for oneself? Who wouldn't want to live the life of their dreams? Changing the world is a goal shared by everyone.

But the bustling lifestyle also has its downsides. A perspective that is seldom discussed or recognized. One with potentially disastrous effects on health, productivity, relationships, community, culture, and the environment.

I'll give you some specific ways in which the hustling culture may backfire on you and others around you:

A lifestyle of constant motion may tire people out. A condition of mental, emotional, and physiological fatigue brought on by prolonged stress is known as burnout. Depression, anxiety, cynicism, apathy, and even suicidal ideation are all symptoms of chronic exhaustion. Everyone is susceptible to burnout if they work too hard for too long without taking breaks. Gallup found that 23% of workers felt burnt out on the job very frequently or constantly, with another 44% reporting feeling burned out on the job sometimes. So around two-thirds of the workforce suffers from exhaustion on the job.

The hustle mentality is harmful to one's health. Overworking may have negative effects on both your physical and emotional well-being. Cancer, diabetes, high blood pressure, and obesity are only some of the chronic disorders to which they may contribute. Additionally, it might lower your immune system, leaving you more vulnerable to sickness.

Overwork also has negative consequences for other areas of one's life, including one's diet, exercise routine, and drug abuse. Stress and boredom may lead people to turn to harmful coping techniques including binge eating, smoking, drinking, and drug use.

Relationships may be damaged by the hustle mentality. Overwork may also have psychological and interpersonal consequences. It has the potential to cause you to withdraw from or disregard your loved ones. It may cause you to miss out on some memorable occasions. It has the potential to separate you from your identity, your principles, and your interests. It has the potential to separate you emotionally from others. Half of the high-earning managers have divorced or split from their spouses, according to Harvard Business School research.

The prevalence of the "hustle culture" might cause societal issues. Overwork also has negative effects on one's family, friends, and neighbors. A culture of rivalry, comparison, and envy may result. It has the potential to create a society based on oppression and inequality. A consumerist mindset may lead to overconsumption and trashing of natural resources. For instance, Oxfam reports that the wealthiest 1% of the population owns more than the rest of the world put together. The World Bank estimates that approximately 700 million people are living in severe poverty. The United Nations estimates that annually 1 billion tons of food are lost or thrown away.

The environment may suffer as a result of the hustle culture. Overexploitation of the Earth's resources is another consequence of overwork. The release of greenhouse gases, as well as your contribution to climate change, might be exacerbated. It may lead to more water use, pollution, and shortage. It may lead to a greater need for energy, more energy waste, and an energy shortage. It may lead to more land being used, more trees being cut down, and lower biodiversity. The Intergovernmental Panel on Climate Change, for one, reports that the average world temperature has risen by 1°C from pre-industrial times due to human activity. More than sixty percent of the world's animal populations have fallen since 1970, according to the World Animal Fund. More than 9 million people die each year due to environmental factors, as reported by the World Health Organization.

These are just a few ways in which participating in the hustle culture may backfire on you and others around you. You can probably think of a lot more. The main issue is that hustling culture is neither long-lasting, wholesome, nor ethical. It's hardly a fulfilling way to spend one's life.

So, what other options do we have? How can we escape the rat race and learn to appreciate the simple things in life?

A Guide to Finding Happiness and Meaning in Everyday Life

I used to believe that the harder you worked, the more meaningful your life would be. I used to think that if I worked hard, stayed busy, and accomplished more, I would finally find success and happiness. For a long time, I believed that my value depended on the results of my efforts and the amount of money I was able to bring in via various means.

Working too much has negative effects on my health, productivity, relationships, community, and environment, as I've discovered the hard way. Too much work may cause burnout, health issues, interpersonal issues, societal issues, and environmental damage, as I've discovered.

Another thing I picked up is that it's possible to work too much and yet not feel satisfied with life. Meaning, purpose, connection, appreciation, pleasure, and love are all things I've discovered that contribute to my sense of satisfaction and happiness.

I realized that it's not about doing more with one's life, but about doing better at what one already does. Work smarter, not harder, to achieve success. Working better, rather than quicker, is the goal.

What I've discovered is that everyone willing to make some adjustments to their routines, outlook, and way of life may achieve a higher quality of life.

And now I want to impart to you the knowledge I have gained.

The following are some suggestions for improving your quality of life:

- Recognize your values. Your values are the guiding lights that illuminate your path through life. They are an expression of your values and a source of inspiration. Having a firm grasp on your guiding principles, or values, may lead to a more fulfilling existence. If honesty is one of your core values, acting honestly toward yourself and others can help you bring that value to fruition and enrich your life.

If being creative is important to you, then finding your unique voice is essential to finding fulfillment in life. The Personal Values Questionnaire, the Values in Action Inventory, and the Values Card Sort are just a few of the many tools and activities available to help you pinpoint your core values. Self-reflection and constructive criticism are additional means of learning more about what you value. Consider querying yourself along these lines: "What are the things that I care about most?" Where do my joy and pride come from? Why do I have such strong emotions? Where do I want my legacy to go?

- Get in touch with your interests and figure out what you're passionate about. They are an expression of your curiosity and passions. By participating in pursuits that excite and delight you, knowing your interests may help you live a fuller life. If music is one of your many interests, cultivating that interest may enrich your life in many ways. If seeing the world is one of your greatest joys, then expanding your horizons will only enrich your life.

The Passion Test, the Passion Wheel, and the Passion Planner are just a few of the activities and resources available to help you zero in on your true interests. Your interests may be better understood via introspection and critique. Questions such, as "What are the things I love doing or learning about?" will help you get started. How can I identify the activities that revitalize me? Consider this: what activities would I do regardless of financial compensation?

- Determine your motivation: Your goal in life, or the reason you came into being, is your purpose. It reveals your innermost drives and what makes you happy. Having a clear sense of why you're here might inspire you to take action that matters to you and the world. By giving your time and money to causes you care about, you may give your life more meaning if one of your reasons is to assist other people.

Writing a book or establishing a company might give your life greater significance if that is one of your goals. The Life Purpose Questionnaire, the Ikigai Diagram, and the Purpose Finder are just a few of the many tools and activities available to help you discover your life's guiding mission. Self-reflection and constructive criticism are further tools for expanding one's understanding of life's meaning. Questions like "What do I want to accomplish in life?" and "What can I offer the world?" are good places to start. In what ways do I want to spend my time? Which activities do I feel most compelled to pursue?

7th
Chapter

Rest More, Wrok Less

7th Chapter

A Romance between Labor and Democracy

To the reader: hello. I'm relieved you haven't abandoned me. You care a lot about finding out how to improve your quality of life. Perhaps you're anticipating some juicy rumors. I promise I won't let you down anyway.

In this section, I'll share with you a romantic tale. A tale of passion between labor and democracy. A love tale that just could make you a better person.

My previous self was a workaholic. I used to think that making a lot of money and advancing in one's job were the two most crucial factors in determining one's level of happiness and success in life. The demands of my job used to cause me to neglect my family and other interests in favor of putting in more time and effort.

I was incorrect.

Work is not as glamorous as people make it out to be. What I've learned is that most of the time, labor is pointless, unfruitful, or unimportant. What I've learned is that work is often pointless, frustrating, and even dangerous.

Work is not everything in life, I realized. I realized that things like love, appreciation, pleasure, and thankfulness are much more important than material possessions.

I realized that working harder is not the key to a happy and fulfilling life, but rather working smarter.

What I've discovered is that everyone willing to make some adjustments to their routines, outlook, and way of life may achieve a higher quality of life.

And now I want to impart to you the knowledge I have gained.

I realized that we don't need to put in as much effort as we do. We may put in much less effort and accomplish the same or even more.

I'll illustrate with an example. Did you know that, according to research, the average person wastes 1.5–3 hours each day on non-work activities? Activities like daydreaming, checking social media, surfing the web, and speaking with colleagues all count as distractions. We could put that time to better use doing anything else.

If we eliminated such times of inactivity, we could shorten our workweek from 40 hours to between 27 and 33. I'd say that's very satisfactory. I agree with you if you believe it's absurd to try to figure out how long we've been working. It's not right for me to just choose figures at random from unrelated research and conduct some quick arithmetic.

But this isn't much crazier than the current method we use to determine how long we put in at work. A small group of individuals at each firm writes our contracts and decides when we work, with the sole constraint being that we can't legally do more than 40 hours per week.

Workers' agitation, revolts, protests, rallies, and other synonyms for furious people clawing it from industry over many decades are the main reasons the figure isn't greater. We would still be working 12-hour days next to kids who should be in school if it weren't for the courageous employees who battled for their rights and dignity.

It's absurd to allow a small group of people to dictate labor requirements, giving in to their demands only when widespread violence threatens social stability. This is ridiculous. This is an unacceptable stage.

There must be a more equitable method to set our work schedules. A strategy that helps us rather than hinders us. A method that prioritizes us above the greed and power of our employers while yet meeting their demands. The method based on the democratic rule rather than the autocratic rule.

In summary, a method that incorporates democracy into economic choices, one that takes into consideration our available resources and our willingness to labor without making us feel like we'll be left behind if we don't sweat like crazy every day. A solution to the problem of people who try to make money off of other people's labor by taking up too much of their spare time. A method that doesn't hinge on how much time we put in on how much the man at the top wants a new watch, ignoring birthdays, funerals, and everything else in between as a result.

Now, this isn't about regressing to a premodern lifestyle that ignores the reality of the immense difficulties and discrimination that premodern cultures faced in the absence of today's technology and social developments. This is about making progress toward a more civilized way of life because modern cultures are capable of achieving both wealth and equality with the help of technology and social advances.

Here are some ways in which you may work smarter:

Identifying the most beneficial option: Working smarter is not about blindly adhering to a set of rules or mimicking the routines of others around you. Workflow customization involves adapting processes to individual tastes, requirements, and aims. You are free to try out various approaches, resources, and techniques before settling on the optimal combination for your needs. To determine what works best for you in terms of productivity, you may, for instance, experiment with various productivity applications, time management strategies, and working spaces.

Use your body's natural rhythms to your advantage by scheduling chores according to how alert you feel. Planning your work around your peak, low, and recovery stages of your natural rhythms and cycles may be quite effective. When you're at your best, you're able to take on the most difficult and time-consuming projects, whereas when you're at your worst, you're better suited to work on regular and boring jobs. The When app, for instance, may help you determine your chronotype and the best times of day for certain tasks.

Working smarter also involves batching operations, or executing many comparable tasks at once. This method may help you save time wasted on unnecessary tasks and streamline your operations. Common actions may be set to repeat at predetermined intervals or cycles. Calls may be grouped in the morning, emails in the afternoon, and reports at the weekend's conclusion, just to name a few examples.

Working smarter often involves delegating work to those who can do them more efficiently or at a lower cost. This method may help you devote more of your efforts to tasks that matter. When you need assistance, don't be afraid to ask for it from your peers, subordinates, or superiors. You might have a virtual assistant take care of your paperwork, have a colleague fill in for you at a meeting, or have a superior act as your project mentor.

Working smarter also involves getting rid of the things that are getting in the way of your concentration on the task at hand. This method might help you focus by quieting your thoughts and blocking out distractions. Avoiding what stresses or depresses you is another way to boost your attitude, motivation, and morale. You may, for instance, use noise-canceling headphones, play soothing music, or disable alerts on your electronic devices.

Well, then, what do we have here?

I suggest that we can reduce our workload and free up more time for fun if we allow people to vote on the issue. The existing work system, which is based on the wishes of a select few at the top and the bounds of the law, is something I have long been critical of. I suggest an improved method of labor that takes into account the wants and requirements of all parties involved as well as the available means.

I also provide a few case studies of people who have increased their output and efficiency by working smarter rather than harder. When I argue that people should work less and rest more, I don't mean that we should revert to a more barbaric era, but rather that we should advance to a more civilized one.

Conclusion

Rest More, Wrok Less

Conclusion.

The Manifesto for a Healthier and Happier Society Can Be Summarized as "Work Less, Rest More, Play More, and Live More."

A review of the basic ideas presented in this book.

Reader,

You probably picked up this book because you're interested in learning more about how to make your life count. Perhaps you need something to read because you're bored. In any case, it's great to have you here.

I'm about to say something that may be seen as quite unconventional, even insane. However, I assure you that it is founded on extensive study, sound reasoning, and common sense. And it has the potential to completely alter your future.

This is it:

Stop working too hard and give yourself a break. Do what you have to do but don't break yourself in the process. You may even end up getting the best results this way.

Please don't dismiss me out of hand or toss out this book just yet. I'm not suggesting you give up your responsibilities and spend all day watching Netflix. I am not advocating shirking your duties, ignoring your family, or giving up on your ambitions.

I think you should cut down on your job schedule and give yourself more time to relax. It benefits your health, productivity, relationships, community, and the environment.

Having doubts? Permit me to provide some evidence.

Work is overrated, that much is certain.

Our society places a premium on hard labor. Having a successful profession and a big income are held up as the pinnacles of achievement in today's society. Everywhere we turn, we hear messages encouraging us to keep our heads down, keep moving forward, and never give up.

What if, though, I told you that working isn't as great as you think it is? What if I told you that most of the time, your efforts at work are pointless, inefficient, or irrelevant? Imagine if I told you that much of your job is pointless, unpleasant, or even destructive.

Put no stock in what I say. Take anthropologist David Graeber's (Bullshit Jobs: A Theory) word for it. He claims in his book that many occupations in today's economy are harmful to people or serve no useful purpose. About a quarter of the workforce, in his estimation, is engaged in what he calls "bullshit jobs," or activity that is so useless or harmful that not even the worker himself can defend them.

Consider this. Just how many bogus occupations are common knowledge among you? What percentage of the workforce do you think does meaningless or unnecessary work? Do you know of any employment opportunities that do not use your strengths and interests? How many occupations do you know of that neither pay the bills nor allow you to pursue your passions?

Perhaps you're working in a bogus profession. Perhaps you spend your days performing menial tasks like copying and pasting information between spreadsheets, answering emails, and writing reports that no one reads. Perhaps you worry that you're using your considerable abilities on matters of little consequence. Maybe you feel like you have no say in your career and no options available to you. Perhaps you're feeling disconnected from the world and that you're not making a difference.

Do you feel this way? And you're not totally off your rocker. You are just caught in an illogical system.

Relaxation time is essential.

Our society looks down on downtime. Leisure time is seen as a waste of time or even a sin. We are led to believe that recreation is a privilege that must be earned. We're always being reminded that our free time is something that has to be managed and regulated.

What if, however, I told you that your time off is not just beneficial, but crucial to your well-being? What if I told you that your free time might be more than just fun? What if I told you that taking time off work to relax is not only good for you, but essential?

Put no stock in what I say. Consider the words of philosopher Bertrand Russell, author of the article "In Praise of Idleness." Leisure time, he writes, is essential to human flourishing. He proposes cutting the length of the workday so that people may spend more time relaxing. In his words:

There is no longer any reason for the bulk of the population to suffer this deprivation; only a foolish asceticism...or an unjust social system...keeps us from enjoying the goods which we have produced.

Consider this. How many different kinds of hobbies and interests do you have? How many different types of entertainment do you find intriguing? How many of your favorite pastimes get your blood pumping? If you weren't being paid, how many of your favorite pastimes would you still participate in?

Perhaps you're an avid music fan, world traveler, or writer. Perhaps you like gardening, crocheting, or playing chess in your spare time. Perhaps you're talented in the kitchen, behind the lens, or at the easel.

You should engage in whatever it is more often. More of it is in your best interest. It benefits your health, productivity, relationships, community, and the environment.

How so? Permit me to provide some evidence.

Downtime improves health.

Taking time for fun has numerous positive effects on health. It can:

- Lessen your anxiety. Taking time for recreation is a great way to de-stress, unwind, and deal with the stresses of daily life. The stress hormone cortisol and other biomarkers may also be lowered. It also helps the immune system so you don't get sick as often.

- Lift people's spirits. Positive feelings like happiness, appreciation, and love are facilitated by leisure time. Happiness and a feeling of direction in life are two other outcomes.

- Boost originality. Free time is a great opportunity to think creatively, try something new, and find solutions to issues. It has been shown to increase brain activity, aid with memory retention, and forestall the onset of dementia.

- Foster development. Spending time doing something you like may help you grow intellectually, professionally, and personally. It has the potential to test you, encourage you, and push you forward toward success.

Downtime improves productivity.

There are several ways in which leisure time may boost job efficiency and quality. It can:

- Increase vitality. Recharging, refreshing, and revitalizing one with leisure time is possible. It may also increase the duration and quality of your sleep, both of which are necessary for peak performance.

- Find your concentration. Spending time relaxing might help you focus by removing mental clutter. Engagement-related factors such as attitude, motivation, and morale may all benefit.

- Boost your abilities. Time spent relaxing may be used as a kind of training that leads to greater proficiency. Finding, developing, and transferring one's abilities is essential for success and may be aided by this.

- Encourage originality. Taking time off may assist with ideation, prototyping, and actualization. Collaboration, communication, and networking are all essential to achieving your goals, and this may help you improve in these areas.

Spending time together in leisure strengthens bonds.

The benefits of leisure to one's social and emotional well-being are many. It can:

- Build bridges. Engaging in leisure activities may improve your social life. As a bonus, it may help you develop the soft skills necessary for a healthy relationship: empathy, trust, and loyalty.

- Widen your perspective. Traveling, meeting new people, and experiencing other cultures are all facilitated by leisure time activities. As a bonus, it may help you develop the traits of openness, curiosity, and variety that are essential to comprehension.

- Find a peaceful solution. Taking time for fun is a great way to unwind, open up, and learn to work with others. It may also help you develop the adaptability, tolerance, and respect that are fundamental to getting along with others.

- Help causes. Spending time doing something you like might motivate you to assist others, rally behind a cause, or sign up for a local organization. Being more self-aware, compassionate, and selfless is good for everyone.

Taking time off is beneficial to the environment.

The positive effects on the environment from leisure activities are many. It can:

- Lessen your intake. Taking time for fun is one way to reduce your ecological footprint. Efficiency, longevity, and conservation are all improved, which is great news for Mother Nature.

- Boost your gratitude. Time spent relaxing may teach you to love the outdoors, value art, and value human life. Experiencing awe, wonder, and thankfulness may also benefit the environment.

- Start something. Spending time relaxing may benefit animal conservation, habitat restoration, and tree planting. Activism, responsibility, and stewardship are all important for the future, and this may help you become more of each.

- Some of the many benefits of leisure time are listed above. You can probably think of a lot more. That's why we shouldn't think of leisure time as something bad, wasteful, or extravagant. Taking time off to relax is important, worthwhile, and admirable.

Stop working too hard and give yourself a break.

Now that I've shown the rationale behind this, I'll explain the steps you need to do to actualize next.

A recap of every major point in this book and more.

Here are some things you can do to cut down on your workload and get more rest:

Talk to your boss or customer and see if you can cut down on your hours or task. If you can convince them that this is in everyone's best interest, you may be amazed at how accommodating they can be. You may suggest working fewer days per week but longer hours per day, working remotely or flexibly, taking an unpaid vacation or a sabbatical, or switching to part-time or project-based employment, among other options.

You may reduce your workload and enjoy more downtime by taking these additional measures:

1. Give part of your work to other people who can perform it more efficiently or for less money. Some of your tasks might be assigned to other companies or individuals. It's also possible to seek assistance from peers, coworkers, and superiors in the workplace. You may have a virtual assistant to help you out with administrative work, have a colleague stand in for you at a meeting, or act as a mentor for your current endeavor.

2. Automate: Make use of technology to carry out some of your most mundane, routine, or low-value operations and procedures. You might save time or effort by making use of several pieces of software or hardware. Systems, templates, and scripts that you make yourself might help you standardize and streamline your job even more. You may use calendar software to keep track of your appointments, a project management tool to monitor your progress, or a pre-written email template to address frequently asked questions.

3. Get rid of the things you're doing that aren't helping you achieve your goals. There's a chance you can cut down on tasks that don't matter or bring much value. You may also get the confidence to decline invitations, requests, and chances that don't fit in with your plans. Stop checking your email every ten minutes; skip a meeting

without an agenda; say no to a task that's beyond your purview.

4. Rank your chores and endeavors in order of priority, urgency, and potential influence. You may be able to zero in on the activities that have the most potential to have an impact on the achievement of your goals. The tasks that aren't as critical to your goals may be delayed, delegated, automated, or eliminated. You may prioritize your work using a variety of techniques, such as the ABCDE Method, the Pareto Principle, or the Eisenhower Matrix.

5. Group related jobs together and do them in batches, saving time and effort. It's possible that you and your friends can get together and do this work all at once. It's possible that you could set up a timetable for recurring jobs and have them run on a set schedule or cycle. You may batch calls in the morning, emails in the afternoon, and reports at the end of the week, to name a few examples.

6. Your tasks and projects should be time-boxed according to their complexity, difficulty, and quality. A certain amount of time might be set aside and strictly enforced for each assignment. It's possible, too, that you'll be able to get started and wrap up each

assignment/project on time. You may, for instance, set a timer for 30 minutes to do research, 60 minutes to write, and 15 minutes to revise.

7. Improve by making the most of your ideal working conditions, routines, and habits as determined by your likes, wants, and aspirations. You could be able to design and keep up a pleasant, functional, and productive office. You could also be capable of creating and sticking to a practical, adaptable, and productive routine. De-cluttering, organizing, and customizing your workspace are all examples of optimization strategies, as are creating, evaluating, and making changes to a schedule, keeping track of, and rewarding positive behavior patterns.

Some of the things you can do to get more sleep and less work done are listed above. You can probably think of a lot more. The notion is that it is feasible and even preferable to reduce one's workload and increase one's leisure time.

Let me now demonstrate what this means in reality once I have shown how this is true and how to make this happen.

Here are some ways in which cutting less on work and increasing your relaxation might benefit your life:

- Reduce your workload and spend more time relaxing alone; doing so may boost your self-care, self-awareness, and freedom of expression. If you want to be happy, healthy, and satisfied, you should spend your free time doing activities that bring you joy. You might, for instance, meditate, read, or keep a diary; you could work out, sleep, or unwind; you could, alternatively, paint, sing, or dance; and so on.

- Reduce your workload and take more time off together with your coworkers and friends to strengthen your ability to communicate, work together, and bond. In your free time, you may contribute to the well-being and satisfaction of others around you. You may express affection in many ways: by talking, listening, or sharing; by helping, supporting, or appreciating; by hugging, kissing, or cuddling.

- You can boost your exploration, education, and contribution if you work less and relax more with the planet. Spending free time helping others is a great way to improve the world. There are many ways to make a difference in the world, including travel, education, and discovery; mentoring and leadership; service and advocacy; and financial support.

These are just a few of how cutting less on work and increasing your relaxation might benefit your life. There are probably a lot more, too. You, your coworkers, and the earth would all benefit from less work and more relaxation.

In that case, why delay any longer?

Let me teach you how to maintain this way of life now that I've shown you why it's true, how to make it happen, and what it looks like in reality.

If you want to work less and relax more, consider these suggestions.

- Think carefully about how you spend your time, both at work and at play. Avoid letting other people tell you how to spend your time. Don't allow other people or things to sway your judgment. Don't allow complacency to hinder you from expanding your horizons. Take the initiative and think carefully about the consequences of your actions. You may, for instance, push yourself by trying new things and welcoming change, or you could assess your alternatives by weighing the benefits and disadvantages and making well-informed judgments.

- Have some leeway in your work and play schedules. Don't restrict your creativity with artificial boundaries. Don't allow setbacks to hinder your progress. Don't allow the pursuit of perfection to steal your pleasure. Instead, practice flexibility, perseverance, and an optimistic outlook on your abilities and potential. You could, for instance, make backup plans, contingency plans, and alternative plans; you could deal with stress, issues, and hurdles; you could accept your errors, learn from them, and move on; and you could enjoy your successes.

- Maintain a sense of equilibrium between your professional and personal life. Work should not take over your life. Don't allow the fun to get in the way of doing what has to be done. Don't allow one part of your life to take precedence over the others. Instead, try to live in a way that is harmonious, integrated, and holistic. There are many ways to improve your quality of life, such as dividing your time between work and play, finding common ground between your professional and personal pursuits, and so on.

- These are just a few suggestions that might help you reduce your workload and enjoy more leisure time. There are probably a lot more, too. The notion is that it is feasible and even preferable to reduce one's workload and increase one's leisure time.

DON'T WORK SO HARD AND HAVE MORE FUN

This is about taking back control of our lives from a system that is squandering our talents and resources. This is about pursuing a life that is rich and rewarding rather than just hectic. How much time do we need to spend at the workplace, Best Buy, AutoZone, and Starbucks? What if we didn't have to work as hard, but yet had enough money to take care of ourselves and our wants? Instead of allowing the market to determine our priorities, what if we had a say in how we spent our time? The gross domestic product (GDP) isn't worth putting people's health and happiness at risk. There is more to life than a job, and we shouldn't have to settle for that as our raison d'être.

It is possible to build a society in which working is not obligatory but voluntary. In which we are not as dependent on digital algorithms and may instead exercise more discretion over the resources we generate and use. Where we can cut down on our hours without worrying about our financial stability. This is a feasible scenario, not a utopian dream. Overwork, stress, and a lack of free time are problems that many individuals are currently facing. There is a growing movement for workplace democracy and more individual agency.

Time to do as we please is a right we should have. in the interest of all people. It might be anything from creating art to listening to music to cooking to mingling to exploring a new city to just unwinding after a long day. We can easily do this. The idea of labor and the powerful institutions that uphold it are the only things standing in the way. We have the power to question and alter their views. We can create a society where effort is valued and respected.

Then why delay any longer?

Stop working too hard and give yourself a break.

Yes, I will repeat myself.

Stop working too hard and give yourself a break.

At, the end of the day we just want more time to spend with our family friends, and our passion. In that case, you should rest more, work less, and play more.

<u>Note</u>

<u>Note</u>

<u>Note</u>

<u>Note</u>

www.ingramcontent.com/pod-product-compliance
Lightning Source LLC
Chambersburg PA
CBHW072329290526
45794CB00002B/801